SPHERE OF SILENCE BROKEN

SPHERE OF SILENCE BROKEN

40 Selected Poems

Lana Wolkonsky

Manufactured in the United States of America
ISBN: 0-9653306-1-3

Library of Congress Catalog Card No.: 96-091547

Dedicated to the light of inspiration
which shines in all of us;
to believe is but to dream
and in so doing
we fulfill our destinies.

CONTENTS

For Nicky, Mamach and Oleg—
my three great teachers of
compassion, love and patience.

BEYOND

Wonder now where love has gone,
It so in splendour fades; leaving
Golden rites and phases
To a motion soft.

Seems that time had slowed tonight—
This purposeful endeavor bare,
Then left but fragrant memory
Upon a mind-swept wave.

Though far from coastlines' gaze this time,
Still through city scapes beyond,
The dreams and visions youth
Once brought remain
To sadness friends.

VIRTUE FOUND

Low, the light this day
That shined these streets
Again and bid farewell;
Wet the morning sun away
To leave all washed,
Forgotten flame refreshed.

Something at this dreary cost,
Reflection in a murky pond—
Look, then lost it too shall
Be among the soaken ashes
Of tomorrow's rain.

When flowing clear, the rivers
Rise and all a gentle smile
Will fade to broken harmony,
Remembered in an earnest way—
The smiles, the tears, the many
Words that were not spoken;
All will meet together then.

While something passes
To another ground, something
We may not yet know;
Something which inside us
Lives and nurtured it
Shall be in time.

Such untamed, mysterious
Desire—be it praised or done;
In moments past recalled itself
A tiny wish; (later grown)
Through work developed,
By endurance finally attained.

It shall (in that most outward
Glory) be united with itself,
As all creation's flow
Caresses to embrace
This virtue found.

A PERFECT GIFT

When in her eyes I see your own—
That wishful glance, that most
Determinate allure; it passes me,
As tranquil gaze on summer
Morning's kind, sweet light.

Such thoughts I have today,
When all eternity can leave
Us blind to this most humble
Magic, this gentle truth.

Gather now your heart and
Let me thank that inner realm,
Known unto you alone as friend;
Because there-in does lie a most
Exquisite soul, a perfect gift.

To just acknowledged be may
Not enough suffice; in this most
Quiet wisdom does your very
Core exist and choose to exit
On such fortunate array—of us.

We, blessed in your humility
May end our days with
Fire in our eye, with madness
Out of reach; with soft,
Assured contentment:

Rich enveloped, most endowed
By your uncompromising soul,
By your forgiving love, by
Your eternal goodness touched.

WE DO

When our minds are left to think,
We leave the day and bound,
Do exit with our souls in line;
Redeem this life within,
Then take our dreams for
Finer balance at true cost.
Assumption's weary try attempts
And fails to falter our will.
We do rehearse this way
About us, longing years away;
Restored on trial's confusion,
Does a celebration rise:
Embracing all an earnest manner
With our passion's heartful song.

DESTINY ALIVE

To be my own caresses and
Tranquil spring's revival night,
To feel the gentle fingers
Of an evening love—
These minutes lone, when
Quiet solitude does reign,
I wash my sorrows dry,
A limp surrender.
Mine, the artist's brush not
Dipped in soft elixir's balm,
Pats bristly coarse along
This chapter's line.
The days are written long
(A mother's care endures)
And fortune swipes with merry
Justice for an unassuming chore.

Still those eyes I see that
Once into my soul did look;
To find the hours in warm
Embrace adoring every state.
Through recollection's
Sentimental key, these
Drawings (seen as such
Remembered gestures)
Now relay through breath,
Through sigh, through
Deep-felt truth kept boxed
Inside this beating chamber.
I am to buy this destiny alive:
To live, to die, to worship what
Upon my own accord does lie.

A TREASURE KNOWING

When into my eye is passed
The softened gaze of innocence,
A cool correction sweeps
Across the evening sky and
Leaves a tear to roll down
Where the music plays.

You look, a treasure knowing,
To the smooth relief of all
The years; the heart is tender
Felt, the harmony of time
Rings on and in a golden
Shadow's edge I see your
Fragrant whisper mouthed.

In awe, such challenges will
Lie ahead; gather now your
Strength, oh tiny warrior—
When dismal promises retreat
May all your valor stay and
Soul uncompromised be.

TODAY

This the day that you
Embark upon a new horizon—
Leave your troubled thoughts
And childhood pleasures
Gone to sweet, such
Unaffected truths.

Challenge now the
Harder realm—of
Knowledge learned,
Of charged ideas,
Of lost experience
To shame.

Wish the dreams on
To yourself, make
Your own desires felt;
With every breath receive
This earth in all her
Splendour, all her fear.

Bless your mind, which
Heart in you alone
The Lord entrusts
And speed you on
Your merry way—
Alas, oh life today!

IN TRIBUTE

On that the day when
Silence sweeps the earth
And her sweet praises
Heard no more, I'll stand
In tribute, teary eyed
To utter not a word!

Then my place will
Buried be, our friendship
Recognized passed; into
The mute triumphant
Winds a hallowed
Heart be hailed.

Until your breath
Uncaptured reigns and
Our times together beat,
A joyous sound shall
Long be heard while
Two caresses fond do
Huddle in each other's flame.

THE HYBRID ROSE

A one, enchanted flower born
On mystic soil, on lost romance's
Final expectation; the vista drawn
Through leaves of rustling,
Silver olive's rhyme and harbor's
Lights beyond that flicker to an
Ancient land, of ruins' night, of
Golden mornings' sacred mist.

That sweet, embracing evening
Scent of foreign lands (now so in
Keeping with this one familiar
Realm) made home and hearth, as
Center to a grace-appeasing dwelling.

Blessed acre ours, that we can
Dream no more; to now embrace
The hour near when it shall
Be the stage for earthly
Resonance and healing.

Quiet corner such— it reaches
Both the heart as true ability to
Think with lucid clarity, with
Unspoiled being and enjoy it's
Fateful hours, its pleasant state,
It's unaffected wind in which
A tale anew is told each hour.
Listen, feel the magic of this
Place; we happy breed that
Can inspired be by such
Alluring, simple pleasures,
By such enamored joy.

WEEKS GO BY

A glory day, the riddled history
And heartfelt pasts are shadowed
By these challenges ahead—
Sometime impossible they seem;
To mend our foes, to gentle our
Haters' will: all such array of
Grandeur takes, to let the weeks go by.

Soften the immune, last gestures
Cradle a most pained remembrance;
What now appear coherent parts of us
Are justly formidable truths.

We (trained to so ignore) relive
Each hurt anew, as shadows roll
Into a moistened mist which now
Absorbed, is our stamp of life:
Not to erase or wash from aged
Skin; nor fade, nor challenge.

This endeavour seems a liking
To the human form: a true and
Complimentary addition; not in
It's seeming freedom, but in love—
That one uniting moment lost,
Then changed, much on occasion
Even hidden in a memory forgotten
With each passing drop of time.

As weeks go by, as strength
Both disappears then surfaces
Again; so often faced with what
We think we know, with what may
Well be done, with what is ours
Not as much as we may so believe—
The tiny lines as the immeasurable
Crevasses (now written 'cross our
Souls) do form a picture just, a
Mold attributed to us alone and when
We will no more, this too may pass.

To leave both dust and ashes
Blown to endless continents, with
Harmonies unheard, with scents
Unknown, not recollected—gone,
Then gone again we too shall be.

THEY DIDN'T KNOW

The mask of death, that put
Upon our children's faces
(Maybe for the last of times
Be kissed) leaves a shiver
Cold; blown streaks atop
The water's edge—
Along the harbor sail.

When these tender graces
That only innocence can hide,
Are ours for the very final moment,
We do part in different spirit; we
Justly challenge our woes.

As harsh truth beats round
Each corner, where then do we
Acknowledged look to long-forgotten
Trust and find a newer
Likeness for this tragic light.

Glittered once, now paled reflection
Turns a metal shoulder, casts a
Watchful eye, passes hardened
Judgment, then gives us back
What we in chance have taken.

Lose the odds and slow collect
The meager winning— taking
Nothing at the toll; so we too,
Such strangers in adventure look
To history, give grace to love,
Acquire freedom for another
Round of captive observation.

Play with words and sadden
Our desire's thrust. Push
Ourselves to go where others
Tamed themselves to challenge;
They didn't know, so onward
(Bound by tribute fair) a joyless
Feat had once again completed
This immeasurable cycle.

Hard cost, battered reason
Lost in dust of years' pursuit;
A tired hand, a summer night:
They blend with quiet calling
To the perfect arch of an
Unreachable and clouded moon.

WE ALONE

Only saddened can we be
By ten-fold clouds that walk
In suits as grey as their
Tremendous souls must feel.

To be anointed by a single
Breath in easy summer rain,
To clearly dissipate a storm
That passed in childhood
Drenched with misery.

Fateful nuisance, trying chore—
Burdens we must all at times
Explore and carry with us
Through all ages.

Troubled, complicated: churning
In the very bowels of our being;
Loosened, free, expelling like
A fragrant evening walk amidst
The green of sacred pride.

We do enjoy alike these ever-
Transient occasions, on which an
Open thought may shut, on which
Our sealed embrace may flee and
Later curse the world around it.

Over in an instant, life; so
Filled with all we know—
Familiar recollections
(Left aside) return each night
To nudge, then beat us.

Lie in hated sweat and
Pure surrender, or revolt:
Resisting tries and torments;
We alone shall always face the
Final hour, though by love be
Blessed, though by worlds embraced.

ONE FISH

She looked at me, a wide-eyed
Monster, human flesh consumed—
In awe of such amazing creatures,
Long have graves astonished been.

The realm of green, soft-misted fragrance,
Loches' perfumes in stillness' heat;
A seasoned challenge faltered grace
(For all the catcher's triumph fades)
When her one gaping eye abolished,
Reaches, then connects this vision line.

Most sacred prize, most harnessed breath—
Now bow a praise, now lift a day;
When in your perfect, shelled attire
You pass this gaze, you still our minds:
Releasing justice with one cast—
Consuming man beyond reprise.

NAMELESS STRANGER

Greys of granite graves have
Passed my vision's ray tonight—
Through you my crevassed
Writer's face, companion strong
In evening's pleasure verse;
Impacted not by sneers of
Praise, you mocked my
Word and lost my gaze.

A HIGHER SONG

When angels seize their flow
And there is but a moment
Of our joy together dropped;
When darkness beats upon my soul
And you, so far shall be—
No longer seen nor heard,
I too shall for an instant perish.

When such sounds of heaven
(Only notes as these can be)
Ring repeated in eternal pleasure;
I will recall your eye, the strength
Of hand, your gift both felt and seen.

Sure it is, that day I'll see
When in heart alone I too
Shall stand and cry as did
All mothers once, for what
No longer in a flash attained can be.

Now play, my muse—muted by
A higher song; and sing to me—
In every movement of your wrist
A kindness long in time I sense shall flee.

Then time again away and free
As only time knows how into
The stillness of another dawn—
Into the transit of another's cause,
Into the dream of someone else's love.

TORMENT OF DEPARTURE

When angels roar outside
The evening's painted sky,
A tranquil road beyond the
Greying life we know;
Shall stand this torment
Of departure—an iron hand,
A shaken grief, the gentle
Rapture of tomorrow's tear
We yet have not endured.

Such sobs and swollen lids
Were only part of past
Assumptions, in forgotten
Years—nights of passion,
Silent days alone; as now
They too would be if
Not for honor's sake,
For honorable produce,
Of an offspring's challenge.

SCORE

Two is yours when
I do floor myself
In honor, face the
World in motor hiss
And ravage wildly
In the night.

A jumpy lot we are,
These once-artistic types
Who hear the withers
Of a lonely stranger as
A petal falls, embracing
Love and silence all in one—
Remaining friends through-out;
At other's cost, what soft expense.

Where souls do rise and
Rip aloud to break that
Coveted allure one had
On eloquent occasions.

To be feared as much, to
Bother with—well now,
In the present filled to
Polished edge; most
Hated course, most
Prized retention—
I oblige and pass this score.

Unkept remains a wash,
A draw, a fragile
Nest of death: this
Leading challenge posed,
This tribute dissipated
In the flesh. Relent and
Drive to charted destination's
Curse; there is no prize tonight
But you, oh dreaded truth—
My seeker such.

A SILENT WORD

Go quick and leave this pair
For some tomorrows later
Heard. I fear to lose the
Gentle understanding had,
Your soft expression gone;
Flown over now to higher
States, to somber truths,
To distant lands.

Fly free, oh creature
Filled with hope; that
In these so-forgotten
Times, there still
Remains a threshold
Such, a priceless insight
Into most-astounding
Recollections and these
Rewards we had are now
But thoughts in passing.

Live well on level,
Conscious ground—
On such recorded,
Clear experience and
Time that so bewilders
Us; free we are to roam
This earth in knowledge
Harvested through mostly
Vacant undertakings:
Go as disappearances do
Pass into the night.

A pristine night so blind,
So rich, so undeniably
A tired night on which we
Pause to only say good-byes;
We know not when we see
Or miss again—we vaporize
Into the mist of time.

We are alluring only to the
Hearts of pleasures found
And to the gentle breezes
That in richness lie alone,
As angels pass and smiles
Are heard no more.

SWEET UNKNOWN

The night is long,
Your deed is done
As so to shallow mercy
I resign and follow—in a
Meeker ground; still, a will
Be found when such mercy
Rings within the heart of man.

In unselfish pleasure
Did my resignation lie,
On a floral bed did
Death arrive; all so
Gaily dressed, all so
Fondly leased for time.

Fare thee well now
Most noble stranger;
I had never known
Your kind to be different
In that subtle field—
Though so wide their talents,
Though so similar their fame.

Innocent denial is my gain
As in your sweet unknown,
As in that ignorance of innocence
Does smile oblivious to me again
And forward in those reigns does
Hold the endless ecstasy of mime.

FINAL CALL

Just when life's
Weighted burdens lift
And all the gentle peace
Is ours for a moment—
(Quiet seen) the
Hammering of most
Unsightly death comes
Near, resurfacing our
Fears; reliving sadly
Buried scenes we
Thought long perished
In a youth forgotten.

Calm, sweet angel
Breath: revive me
Now—as winter passes
Into spring and healed
Become the wounds
Of treasured loves.

Let not the face of
Sour gloom anticipate
Its presence yet;
The lamb saved for
Tomorrow's angry
Test as we, all human
Enterprises are and
Nesting clubs for
Timid resource large.

Wake not the lithe,
Sweet beast of hunger
Lest he roars—a tame
Reflection just, may be
The stolen trust we lost
Along the roads of pain.

Do not forget
The stones we
Threw were later
Thrown at us and
As we wiped the
Bloodied dirt,
Again upon our
Faces written was
Regret untold and
Uncorrected errors
We could not exude
From records past.

Now face alone
This final call,
Rise tall in wake
Of justice catching
Grief—do not try
To humble feathers
Fluffed in burned
Remains and
Treasured ruins;
Bleed us dry until
We so dismissed
Are there to speak
In no relief, to live—
No chore; so fancy
Our wills and try
In peace to finish.

COMMITTED LOVE

This wondrous art, which
So prolonged will one day
Reign eternal in our souls—
To sleep and dream the
Realm once known to us
In times now passed,
Yet never gone.

These harlots still a piece
Of tender life exude, as we
Are all a bit of them inside.

Those forward years, in
Ending triumph; darkened
Pits did share—in blackness
Now to still and wish, to
Not arise, to weep no more.

When only rested in a minute
Instant seemed, where all life's
Treasures then adorned—as
One, forgiven blessing seemed
To pray for their forever rest.

Oh chalice hard, that each
Forgetful year may pass and
Still not wipe complete this
Treacherous endeavour for a
Lifetime branded in your being.

That drink I must alone ingest
And somehow swallow as a
Tax anew—your care, such
Precious memories it carries.

Though it seemed in trying
Measure to reveal, yet not;
Such wandering and reckless
Cruising now dismissed.

Rip wide the wound of love
And pour an acid into flame,
To eat away these endless fears
Your dedication brings:

When null I am to someone else's
Comfort, when void become our
Reputations in a lingering relation.

I too may once dismissed become,
But newer tries have challenged
Such vocations: the core continuation
Brings; to never let true honor rest again;

To feast the trembling eye and heart
On this one-decade knot; this,
Brotherly, committed love.

TONIGHT YOU SLEEP

When all the world
To sleep does go
And my sweet angel
Breath upon me sings,
To dreams I turn a
Shadowed death;
To rise, to fall
Upon this earth.

A humble dwelling
Wipes this tender
Flesh, this solemn kiss—
To fret, to steal a winter's
Memory in casting summer's
Reel—the catch of youth,
The fire's feel I throw
To lofty swells
In aging grief.

Remember me
Tomorrow, when
The autumn winds
Will blow my
Softened light's
Request and then
Replenished, my
Endeavours reap
And swallow what
An early tide
Brought in.

MADE OF FLESH

A funny thing—
We share the sand
As children's laughter
Changes our smiles to
Tears and weaves it's way
To unknown resource.
None have yet to see
The promised future
Traded free, nor
Drink the tender
Cup of youth;
Dry these wet ambitions,
Soak a perfumed soil—
To harvest drained
Illusion's way:
Initials changed, a key
To hearts that never
Opened, now remain
A photographed recall
And we are only
Made of flesh—to
Perish as the gentle
Rains of summer pass,
Gallant as a stranger.

PURITY DIVINE

Hard-born hatred; practiced,
Then rehearsed in falling days,
In failing grace—on me bestowed
Like ashes: blow these years,
Remember as a perished beat
This one, blatant recourse.

Cursed error, trying times which
Follow in the death of night—a
Tranquil sleep, a favored, linen sheet
And purity divine, which in a
Bluish haze does pass on me, then
Leave the moment void of pleasure.

Push and plea; tremble at the gate
Of sorrow left unfed, unheard—
Now fill these terrible suspicions
With relief and live this honor flat.

A neutral time, a shaken grief
Revived, remembered and torn
From life as bitter remedies are
Dropped, as perseverance
Holds its cost.

Wild smile of lost ambitions;
Evil mind, reverted chord of
Faith unjust—do sing to me in
Steely harmony of time, do lose
Me to you truest, hard condition.

Let the angels love another
Voice of reason and believe
My naked will; just cause,
Ample twist and lassoed tale
Re-chewed and told again—
The verse remains, the taste
Disdained attests to hours lost
On empty promises and shattered
Chains of aggravations' action.

Lost traditions, honored faith—
Pray now in midnight chill for
Soft ascensions and a newfound
Peace to give away.

NONE DENIED

The culmination of ideas changed
And it's expression such, to bleak
Reverberations is reduced.

In this simplicity an honor reigns,
As we, the harvesters of change,
Still breed. Bow low, this praise
For it now new has taken
Over ground before revered.

And we to ashes burn our triumphs
There is none to challenge, none denied—
A loose anticipation with a fervor rises;
Read and see what monuments to
Phrases can one build.

How names will then exchange
Their very cores when silenced
Strangers state their bliss—
Quiet anguish fills the pores of
Vacant time, where all sweet
Undertakers dwelled.

Living death, we know not our
Transgressions yet; when gentle
Oils may wipe our days and
Lubricate the senses.

Free to think, this action takes
Where looming cry may burn—
What poetry is this that in the
Modern verse is heard.

HONOR'S WILL

There, in midst of past's sweet
Glory, beauty lies concealed by
Fame and all the precedent of
Day's endeavours justly done.

The herald's scream, the brow's
Hard whisper—so they resonate
In shame; when simple tribute
Pays no honor to a minimal salute.

Angry lives, far arrangements treat
This pardon with appeal—in a time
When fallen angels praises sing.

To me who sees no beauty
In that promise—spend
The night in reverence of such
Remembrance, beauty made; that
True, no honor challenged.

Yet still your gaze upon these
Matters rests and when that weary
Death, whose look, whose breath
Upon me takes; when venues change
A sudden quest to fret, it may
Indeed be ours: to intrigue the
Senses, to indulge the eye.

Feast on me, oh tranquil stranger
Who has now inhabited my life.
As I so willing give (in order)
A serene observance felt.

LIQUID PLEASURE

Tomorrow you will once again
Depart and leave me in this
Sweet night's liquid pleasure.
With the harvest moons and
Harboured dreams that pass
And pass again each year;
Never will I know their
Simple meaning, watch them
Gather, flock and tear.

Not impartial to our journals,
Still a stranger I remain.
God-forsaken for a moment,
Time will heal this fastened
Scorn or be swallowed by
Lessons learned, ignored
In future's will.

While they sleep, my
Angel treasures, I am
Born to witness life—
In it's power, in it's teaching:
All alone as wicked force
Will bathe our worries,
Try our witness—
Soft caresses our woes.

UNFORGIVING PASS

Broken homes and broken dreams,
Broken promises it seems are my
Generation's lost forgiveness, are
These limbs and knees—to them
We bend and scorch our stolen years.

Time will heal no burdens lost,
Unfulfilled emotions passed; leave
The humble task of sorrow on a
Rosy-lipped, well thought-out kiss.

Fall from grace to challenge more
Of these most unattributable fears.
Wrap the world in caring cause,
Seal it's future in a journalistic
Clause and fight this fight alone—
The anger that we face is
Real, not our own.

Then we, like ship lights in the dark:
Try and trail, sweep then drown
In moments by a vivid shore.
Fail again and loose the war against
The love our mothers bore.

There is no answer to this case
That in the stillness bare does
Sound and so reverberate it seems
A toil. Try and fail, toss to change
Direction on the unforgiving pass.

ON A CROSS-TOWN STREET

The smell: New York; so wry,
So laced with autumn sweetness
Dry and ready as a lone lark
Heaven Breathes—a judgment
Fair (We fancy folk do fathom) as
The smell of soft indulgence pure.

The sound, to beat—oh youth
She said it was, but I know better;
True—it is the breeze I love and
Loved in nights long passed,
Laced with perfumed soil and
Silence: that poisoned gas, that
Very core of all-night splendour;
When conversations full I had
(That lasted 'till a dawn anew)
Had sprung and left the breathing
Passion vacant for a lifetime.

You—people of this past I sing
In chords and verse unknown;
In muted moments, when the
Diesel passes on a cross-town street,
Again I find myself in harmony
With nature: as dreamers pass and
I, alone will sing my final praises.

MOON WALK

Far—in fields of amber;
Where a lavender aroma and
A chilling mist do rise together:
A connection perfect in the
Splendid landscape young.

A face of love, the passion course
(Forgotten long) to these perfumed,
Sweet grasses goes; and we—
In this aroma walked a dawn to see,
To sleep the day, to rage the night.

The moistened flesh, the
Dampened hay—all live
In corner's memory,
In soul's amazing recollection,
In each detailed verse.

Where unknown villages
Were neared amidst the
Soft and almost dream-like
Sounds: the cows in pasture,
As the rattle of a harnessed
Steer; the world alone then
Stood, when time was limitless,
When reason short was ours.

The wetness through our shoes did
Seep on that "moon walk," on that
Un-named hill: in time now stored,
In custody of promise kept.

NONE SO FEW

Tomorrow—when the enemy
Will face a stare to pierce the
Skin, a morning bare in winter glory
Stands; the angel hearts may sing and
Find their solace in an ancient silence.
Just as gentleness is gone, anguish too
Might perish—leaving voices' echo
In a yet-uncharted track. Bearing
Witness to perception is the giver's
Eye—to each a multitude of talent given,
None so few, as none so weak will
Compensate each other's losses.

DESERVED FATE

What to shining hearts is this
That passes by on autumn nights
Without a recollection, leaving
Transit thrown to those who
Spend their minutes precious
In a fleeing glance.

What to faded years is this
That smiles forgotten in an
Endless future—darkness
Wild, unknown. What to
Working hands is this that
Trembles in an early frost
And loses life too soon to
Such unhappy consequence.

What to hopeless dreaming
Can a consolation be when
Yellow moons and purple
Stars appear on velvet skies;
We sketch these memories
(In fact to keep) and say
Farewell, deserved fate.

What to honour's gaze
As old, intensified
Appearance holds—does
Keep a sour note concealed,
Does turn a wish to gold.

ETERNAL PROMISE

There is an hour when the sun does
Break inside a tainted glass and
Beam with brightness such, that
Man's illuminated lights seem fey
Compared to glory's image strong.

Quiet sits the lonely train of thought
Beyond the concrete walls and children's
Painted halls of soft remembrance; there,
Within this monument to truth, a voice
May rise in singled harmony to sing the
Hymns of snow-layed days and frequent
Promises left trapped on a city's streets.

Bright yellow beams and David's star
Within the world we know are left asunder—
Why now in splendid silence, with only
Muted talk (the voices of tomorrows'
Flock do ring) does angled image of
A lonely man; led off to desperation,
Shine a tremor in this complicated heart.

May Christmas come again and soft adorn
These graces as each station's platform
Trembles in the frost of morning darkness.
Standing cold, awaiting exile to the
Worker's land of day, we have
No words to pray for lost endeavours,
Lost defeats—only time can heal these
Mild disgraces and receive a new-found King.

When in blue, a cross will lay; in front of
Challenges proposed and voided—
Young anticipation voices every longing,
Every try. We will bury these forgotten
Milestones as the new breed rises to this
Shimmering of spring; long the winds of
Autumn's nervous energy do pass—
Tranquil patted in the snows
Of our eternal promise.

ONE THING OUT

When rains did fall like
Tears on flavoured hills
From swollen skies; while
Now I look, to see a perfect
Painted sheet of such exquisite lights:
A pink perfection hailed in blue—
The unity of souls unite on this,
A satin canvas told in dreams away
(Into a midnight void of silence).
Serve unearthly sights to me
On liquid trays with icy smiles and
Tender flesh to keep this one thing out.

Horned emotion, forked response—
What liberation holds an
Oceanic vent of freedom bound,
Of mists anointed by a palette sweet
On picture dreams—do close these
Shutters strong that peek in
Untold pleasure on the phantom hills,
The mossy turf; the lost, abandoned
Fields of future harvest.

Bless this night that comes upon
Us as the distant light upon a slate
Horizon fades; to hold a treason in
Good will and challenge hearts that
Never change to our condition—
Streak the red, then close our
Day with clean emotion, with
A patterned spray of salty
Mist and running time away.

OF FAMILY

Across the darkened tracks,
Beyond the bus depot where
Arise, the fumes arrived in tow—
A single dash to freedom
Now a latent thought;
On summer nights, in
Early snows, in rain,
In sun, in even stubborn will
I came to walk that way:
Along my Ocean Avenue
To turquoise silence;
To a warmed soup,
To making dinner for myself,
To some senses lost: of family.

The fear transpired and
The deaths recalled—
The third one out was Dad;
Upon his tombstone snow
Did fall and many seasons
Passed without a visit.
Parks and lakes and summers hot,
The sweat recalled on
Short-sleeved shirts—
I write my blood upon this wall;
In humble heart do I surrender.

What in shared emotion
As in sleep's sweet memory
Did dream again of youth
So pure, so hard.
Now lie, now fade,
Now promise none—
No more and in the
Pageantry of vividness
All signs do stop, all
Roads do burn in
Frequent love; in tarnished,
Long anticipation.

Dread not when in turn
Those visits seem
Salutes to fame, to
Ill misunderstandings:
As beads and rings
In drawers display—
Those same in turn will pass;
Calling but another by that name.

So try, unleash those days to me,
Of ice cream stands and bottled milk—
The smell of ocean-side resorts
And carmel corn. Her glasses thick,
Oh mother of my mother (blind in
Stumbling night) did cry upon her knees
For me—without response, without an answer.

My anguish can today acknowledged be,
When burned I am in torrent tears
And acid dreams. As he in front of me
Has passed this stage and freed
Examination such to time, to
Speech, to awkward silence;
To those long, pushed conversations
That would swim in grief—that had
Ended in this bond of truth.

Each limit on a candied life
Can stray and so alone remain
With ghosts of love to gently
Haunt them, bleed them dry;
But when a flow of cast recall
Still hungers for a second youth
(A freedom's chance) the muse
Can live eternal in a baseball field:
The crowds no more, the lights away—
The voices louder than before,
The glare—more bright.

So sip your soup now cold
And bury friends this time;
As they remain the family of
Life to us, the family of truth
And in their hearts the
Family of flesh rides
Equal in the night.

BEYOND REPRISAL

There is no time to heed,
For short the day and
Long the silence thus—
An ending promise fades
In grey, transparent fumes;
In lost vocation.

So sleep in tact—
Again a dawn away;
Do practice this my malice,
Friend: to close the choice
But leave the void dismissed
Beyond reprisal.

FINAL GRIEVANCE

This is the face that looks at you
In plain, white ghostly light—
(As tears that roll translucent
Down these cheeks) and says
Farewell to angel hearts, as
To the promises once broken
Under starry, black, eternal skies;
Remember youth in all its
Fair destruction, wasted nights
(Awake in soft displeasure)
And your crescent kiss,
Once placed articulately
On these lips of death alive.

Now bewildered in such fear,
The game is lost in jest—
A final grievance bare to
End a wasteful tale of
Loud rampage and buried
Talents. No excavation can
Now justify its living—this
Untreated shame; this sole,
Disgraced repute. How in
A ringing silence does the
Pain proclaim itself undone;
When to the very last effect of
Readiness a quiet bow is
Made at last; alas! these gentle
Breaths of hope do sound so true.

BRAVE NEW YORK

Creeping, like the endless spirit of
A flowing life—these radiant reds
And brilliant orange punches blind
With yellow fibers in an autumn sun;
The mist of memory still rolls, still
Reaches it's invisible, yet silky fingers
Through these trees and into this
Most present soul of truth.

Painted radiance in heated bloom—
These motor birds and those old-
Fashioned seagulls cry; they launch
Themselves so perfectly atop the glass
Reflection of the city's reservoir—
Oh brave New York, in your
Intoxicable splendour I profess
My faith to match your steely will;

Your spirit, your painted sheathes
Of gold that lie now sprinkled
On this concrete carpet, a now-
Embroidered rug of rock most
Black and grey. Raise high your
Perfumed stench of diesel oil's
Delights and perforate the nostrils
Bare of weakened flesh, of watered-
Down emotion's feeble blood.

In this perpetual revival, this
Non-ending fear, this broad
Excitement and confused pride
I live and honor life for you:
My favoured residence of youth,
My home for freed, alluring talk—
My glorified then humbled ghetto of a life.

IN QUIET GLORY

The beauty of a morning,
When the sun fills up a room—
And there is no more worry
For this brief iota, for this
Savoured hour; we can free
Ourselves of time, to simply
Watch the movement of a
Delicate dawn's rays make
It's way on high. In silent,
Muted verse our history is
Told, received—there, in
Quiet glory, sank the truths
Of gentler folk, of angel flutter
And a princely rhyme.

Now they too have angered,
Raised and changed themselves
So to accommodate these times
Of fight and righteousness—in
Real emotion, there is no more
Will than there is power to undo
These things once written.

We transform ourselves to fly
A different pattern, yet the race
Remains un-won, as there are
No clear champions; merely
In attire (their spirit vanished
For a growing cause) these
Stately rebels reach and fall
In memory's remembrance.
Then we no more, then other
Days are won and on the
Sweet, uncharted promises
Our truths revive themselves
And life through us: in pristine
Resurrection goes!

FRONT PASSING

That those of us who see—
To witness these amazing sights
Of boundless light and ancient will,
Of radiant punch, of night's
Illumination still (on wet
And drizzled streets) that
Glow in cold, white burn;
That trace our youth's lost
Magic, that with anger do
Compare in smoke stacks
Rising from a Europe's
Flavour lost along the
Road to freedom past.

Still perfect images be caught
In moments as this terrible
Illusion fades, as gold in
Painted color—as a dream
Does set itself before our eye
And make us tremble from it's
Boundless beauty, just as sense
Can touch those willing darknesses
In which the rain can fall invisible.

It, now a screen of Vincent's
Brush upon a country field—
Becomes the soft, ethereal
Magnificence which like a
Fairytale falls down upon the
Rotting earth; exuding musky
Dirt and fragrant soil. Such
Treasures it becomes like
Jewels fair, a lovely vision on
A morning so poetic—when the
Lights of night still shine amid the
Gleaming rays and rainbow's arch.

Again it reaches to the still
Creations and amazingly it
Colors-in with autumn's
Glory lights—now sinking
In the gull's most velvety
Pond rest; this too must go
From us—as so it does
To leave a common,
Rainy day be ours.

It was a morning savoured in
The hardened will of mankind's
Dream—awake in such abounding
Pleasure, does it ease our hearts
To think it gone; to once re-visit
This sweet breath of earthly picture
Fair: dismissed, yet captured in the
Heart's forgiving eye, its boundless
Sight. The vision rests again renowned,
Again alive as if it were for all eternity with us.

Sphere of Silence Broken was designed and printed in an edition of five hundred copies by The Oliphant Press, New York City. It is set in Bulmer type, with headlines in Neuland. All papers used in the book are recycled.